The Incredible Human Body Activity Book™

Editor: Victoria England
Editorial assistant: Mark Williams

Published in Great Britain in MMXIV by
Scribo, a division of Book House, an imprint of
The Salariya Book Company Ltd
25 Marlborough Place, Brighton BN1 1UB
www.salariya.co m

PB ISBN-13: 978-1-908973-63-4

3 5 7 9 8 6 4

A CIP catalogue record for this book is available
from the British Library.
Printed and bound in China.
Printed on paper from sustainable sources.
Reprinted in MMXVIII.

Visit
www.salariya.com

for our online
catalogue and **free**
interactive web books!

PAPER FROM
SUSTAINABLE
FORESTS

The Incredible Human Body Activity Book

Packed with facts, games and experiments!

by Jen Green

illustrated by

David Antram

SCRIBO

How tall are you?

Measure your height and draw yourself between the two figures.

An adult's height is eight times the size of the head.

A baby's height is four times the size of its head.

How many times does your head fit into your height?

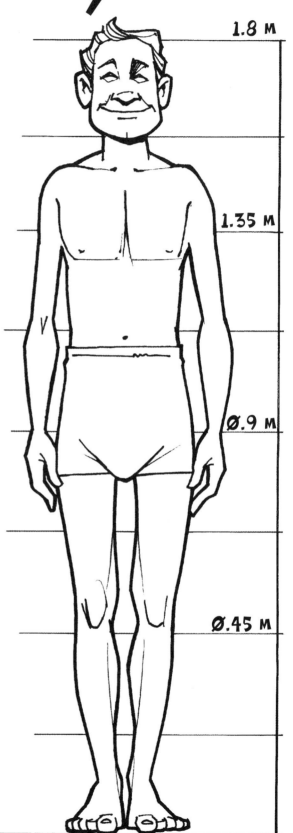

1.8 M

1.35 M

Ø.9 M

Ø.45 M

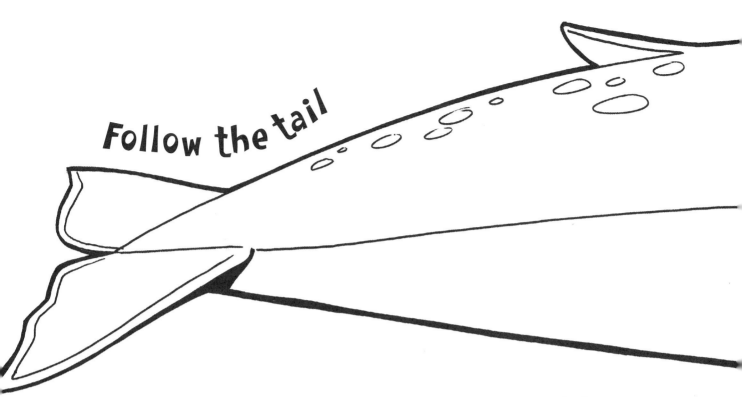

Follow the tail

Biggest and smallest

The tallest man who ever lived, American Robert Wadlow, was 2.72 m.

Average human 1.65 m.

Chandra Bahadur Dangi of Nepal is the shortest man, Ø.55 m.

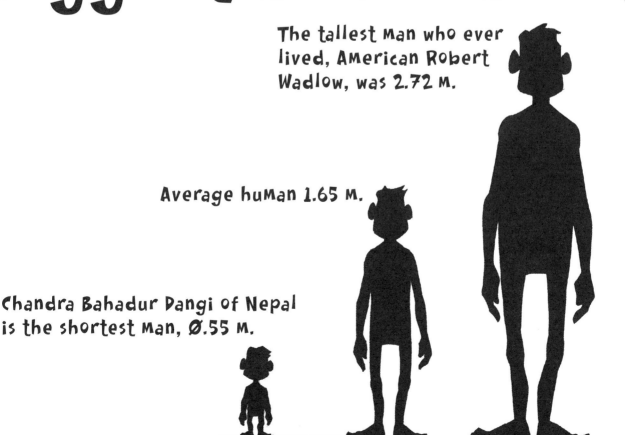

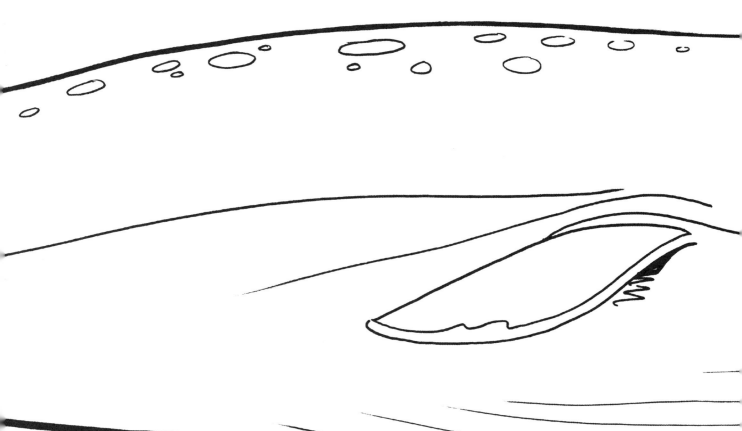

colour the picture

Animal sizes
An elephant stands twice as tall as a human, but the dinosaur *T rex* was over four times taller. Eighteen humans lying head to toe would measure as long as a blue whale.

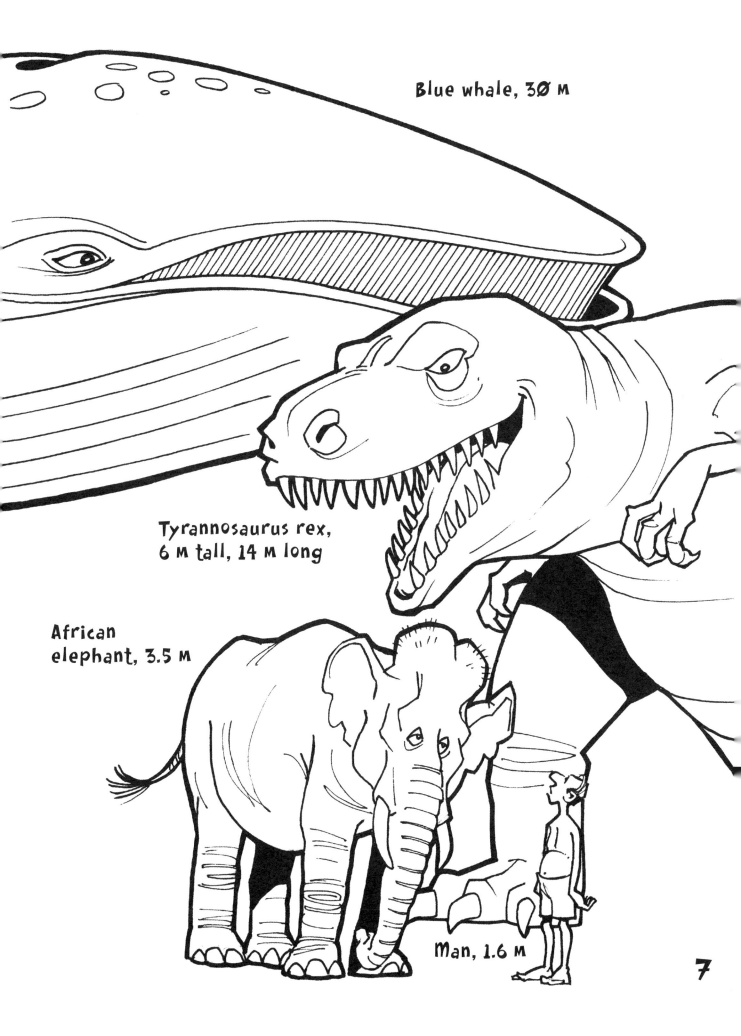

Blue whale, 30 M

Tyrannosaurus rex,
6 M tall, 14 M long

African
elephant, 3.5 M

Man, 1.6 M

7

Hair

Hair protects your head and keeps you warm. Hair can be dark, fair or ginger, and straight, wavy or curly.

Tiny hairs grow all over your skin, except on your lips, the palms of your hands and the soles of your feet.

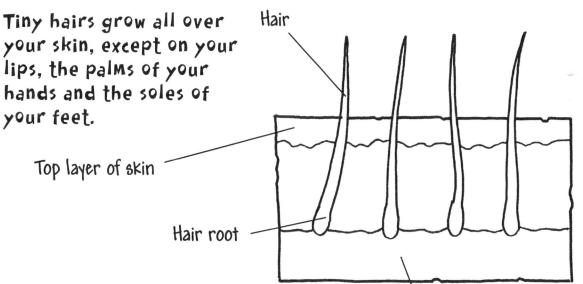

Hair

Top layer of skin

Hair root

Layer of fat to help keep your body warm.

Did you know?
Hairs grow from living roots in the lower layer of skin. But the long hairs you see on your head are dead.

Draw hair on these people.

Match the organs

1. Filters bad stuff out of your blood and turns it into wee.

KidNey

----

2. Runs the whole of your body from your head.

----

3. Long tubes that absorb the goodness from the food you eat.

----

4. Used for breathing air in and out.

HEART

PANCREAS

SPLEEN

colour the pictures

5. Pumps your blood around your body.

----

6. Uses acid to break down your food.

----

7. Cleans and stores your blood.

----

8. Makes special chemicals to keep you healthy.

BRAIN

KIDNEY

STOMACH

INTESTINES

LUNGS

Answers to the puzzles begin on page 92.

Make a Monster

Frankenstein is a famous horror story written by Mary Shelley. It was published in 1818.

Victor Frankenstein was a scientist who built a monster from dead body parts. He meant it to be beautiful but the result was hideous!

Play Frankenstein and design your own monster. You can use human or animal body parts.

My monster

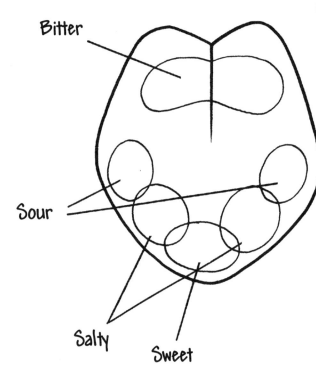

Bitter

Sour

Salty

Sweet

Taste test

Taste and smell are two of your five main senses.

Your senses of smell and taste can warn you of danger, such as smoke from a fire, or rotten food.

Different parts of your tongue pick up four main tastes: sweet, sour, salty and bitter.

Identifying different foods is tricky if you can't see them. Blindfold your friends and see if they can identify foods from just the smell and taste.

See who does best by putting a cross or tick by their result.

	Person 1	Person 2	Person 3	Person 4
Strawberry	—	—	—	—
Cucumber	—	—	—	—
Chocolate	—	—	—	—
	—	—	—	—
	—	—	—	—
	—	—	—	—
	—	—	—	—
	—	—	—	—
	—	—	—	—
	—	—	—	—

Breaking down food

Food takes over a day to pass right through your body.

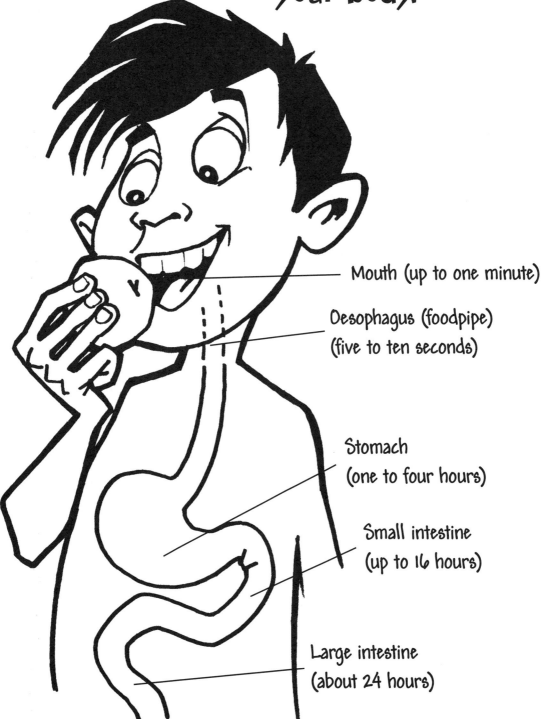

Mouth (up to one minute)

Oesophagus (foodpipe) (five to ten seconds)

Stomach (one to four hours)

Small intestine (up to 16 hours)

Large intestine (about 24 hours)

Know your food

A healthy diet contains lots of different foods. Proteins such as fish build bones and muscles. Carbohydrates such as rice provide energy. Fruit and vegetables contain vitamins, minerals and also fibre, which helps with digestion. Eating too many sugary or fatty foods such as sweets and crisps isn't good for you.

Match the food on the left to the correct food type on the right

Bread, pasta, rice, cereal	Protein
Milk, yogurt, cheese	Fat and sugar
Meat, fish, eggs, nuts, beans	Calcium
Fruit and vegetables	Carbohydrates
Chips, sweets, etc...	Vitamins and minerals

How you see

Light passes through a hole called the pupil, in the coloured part of your eye. It passes through the lens which focuses it on the retina at the back of the eye. This sends signals via nerves to your brain.

Retina

Optic Nerve

Pupil

Lens

Image appears upside down on retina

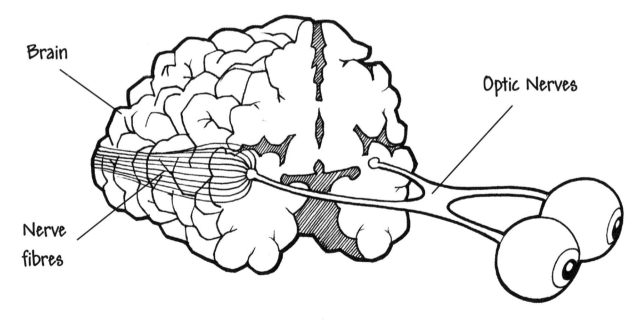

Brain

Optic Nerves

Nerve fibres

colour the pictures

Tricking the eye

Look at this picture for a minute or two. Then close your eyes. You should see an image of the skull even though your eyes are closed.

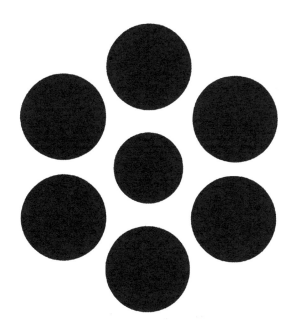

Look at the circles in the centre. Which looks bigger? Now measure them with a ruler.

More eye trickery

Look at the parallel lines in these drawings. They appear to bend, though in fact they are straight.

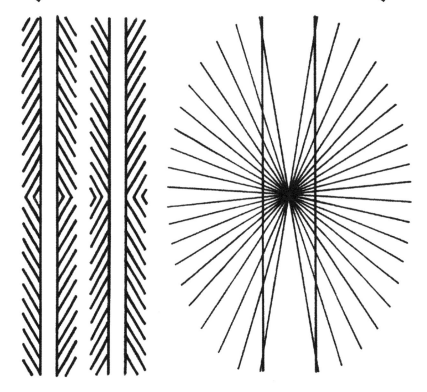

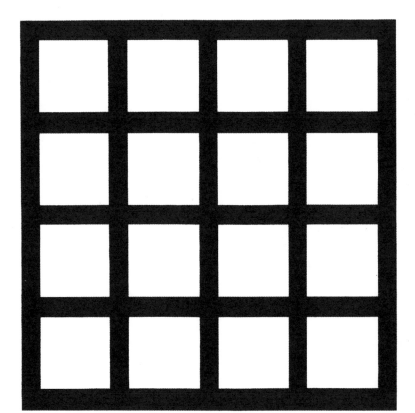

When you stare at the white squares, do pale blobs appear in the corners?

When you stare at the black squares, grey blobs appear in the corners.

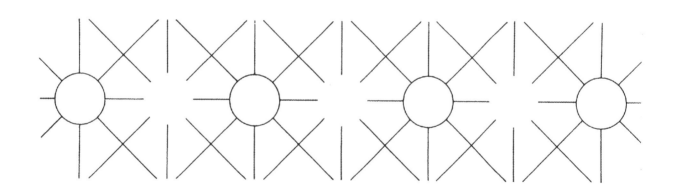

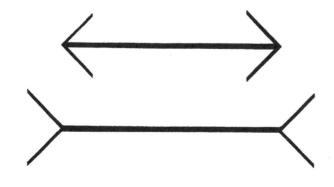

Which look brighter, the circles enclosed by black lines, or the unenclosed circles at the centre of the crossed lines?

Which of the two horizontal lines looks longer? Now measure them with a ruler.

Breathing

Vital oxygen enters the body via the lungs. Air passes down your windpipe into your lungs, which contain many small airways.

Find the route down the windpipe into the lungs.

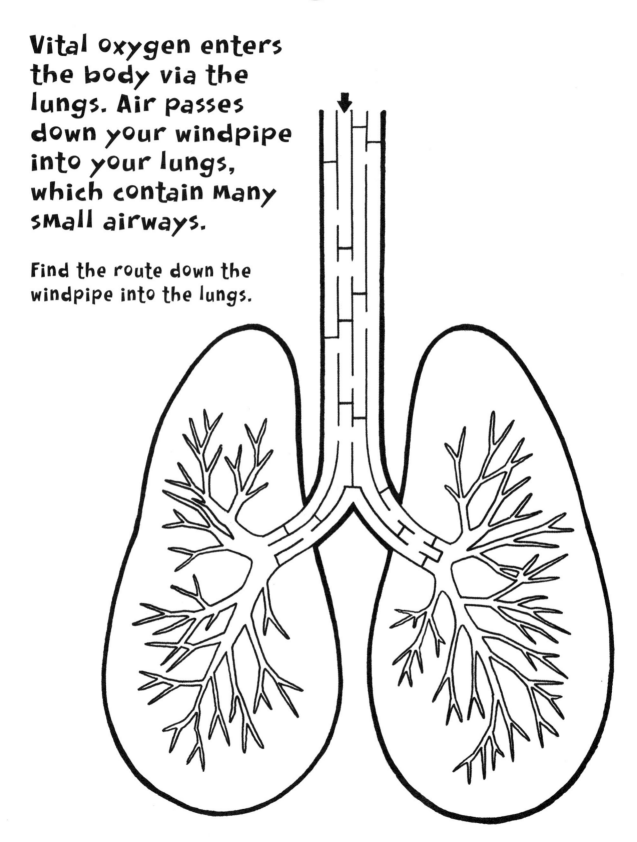

How much air do you have in your lungs? Take a deep breath and empty your lungs into a balloon.

The air you breathe out is warm and moist. Breathe onto a mirror and see what happens. Now rinse out your mouth with cold water and try again.

Digestive puzzle

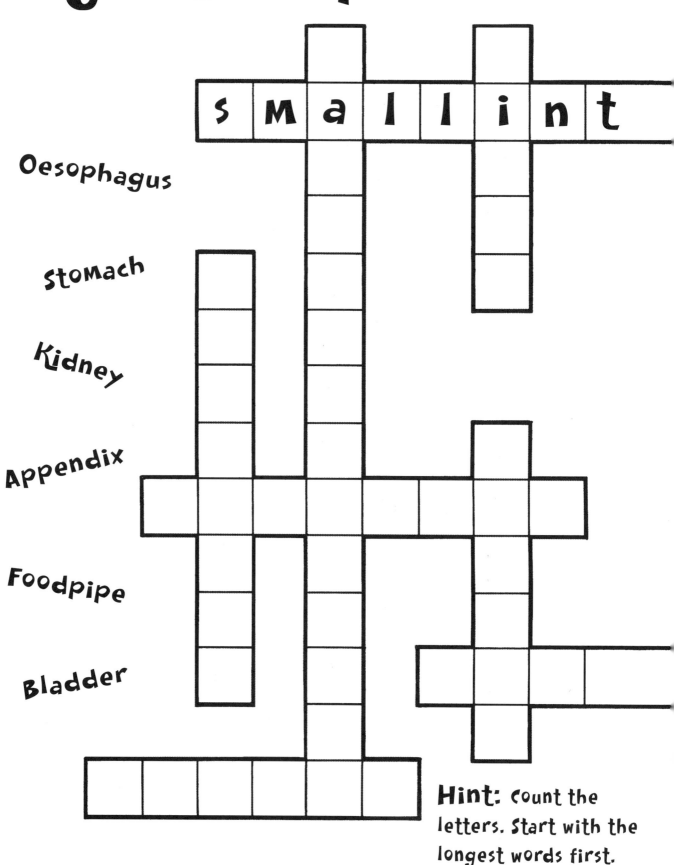

s m a l l i n t

Oesophagus

Stomach

Kidney

Appendix

Foodpipe

Bladder

Hint: Count the letters. Start with the longest words first.

Place these words for parts of the digestive system in the grid.

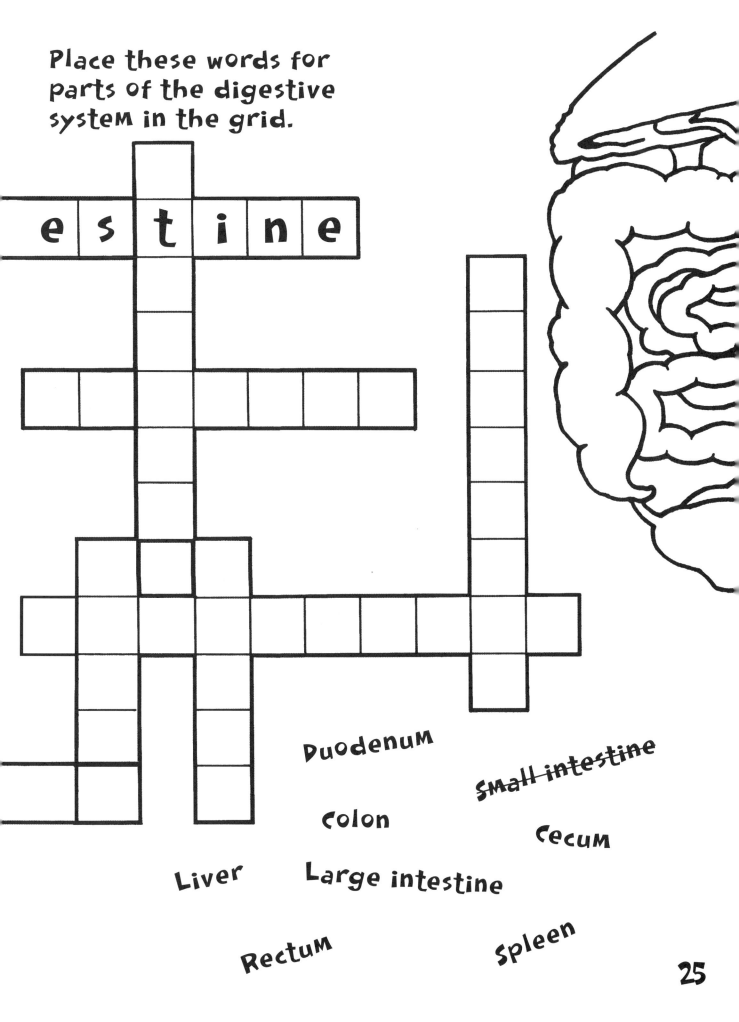

e s t i n e

Duodenum

Small intestine

Colon

Cecum

Liver

Large intestine

Rectum

Spleen

25

Sudoku puzzle

Test your brains with this Sudoku puzzle! Each row, column and 2 by 2 square must have all four numbers.

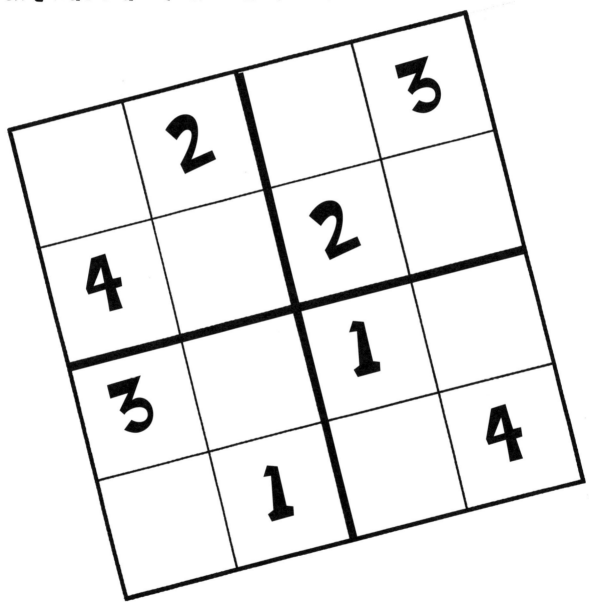

Digestive Maze

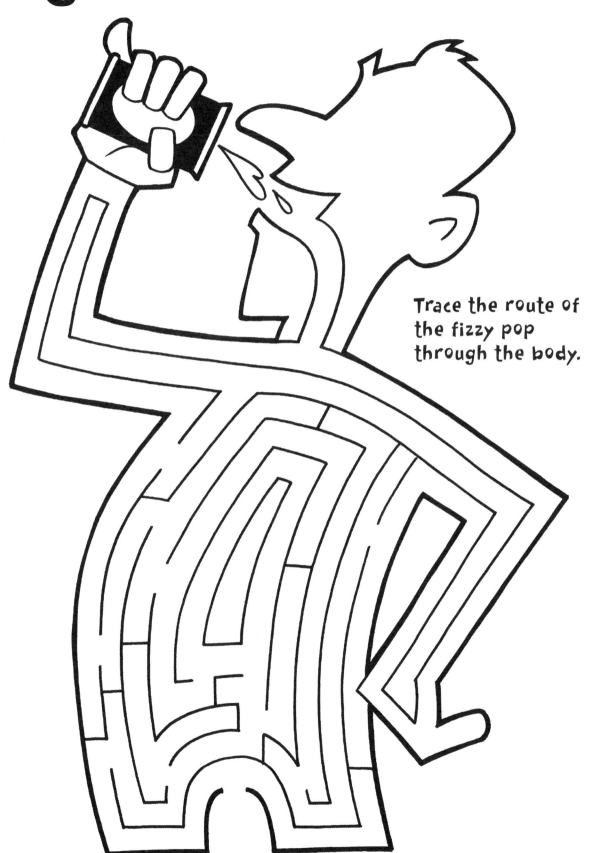

Trace the route of the fizzy pop through the body.

Digestive teaser

Your digestive system breaks down your food and absorbs the goodness. The rest is waste!

How many words can you make out of the letters from DIGESTIVE SYSTEM?

DIGESTIVE SYSTEM

GIVE

TEST

Drawing portraits

No two people look exactly alike – even identical twins are slightly different!

Is your hair straight or curly? What colour are your eyes? What shape is your nose? Do you have freckles?

Study your face in a mirror and draw it.

Draw one of your friends.

Now draw another friend.
Can your friends recognise
each other from the drawings?

Facial expressions

Fit these words to the expressions on the faces.

ANGRY   **FRIGHTENED**
LAUGHING   **SMILING**
TIRED   **ALARMED**
GIGGLY

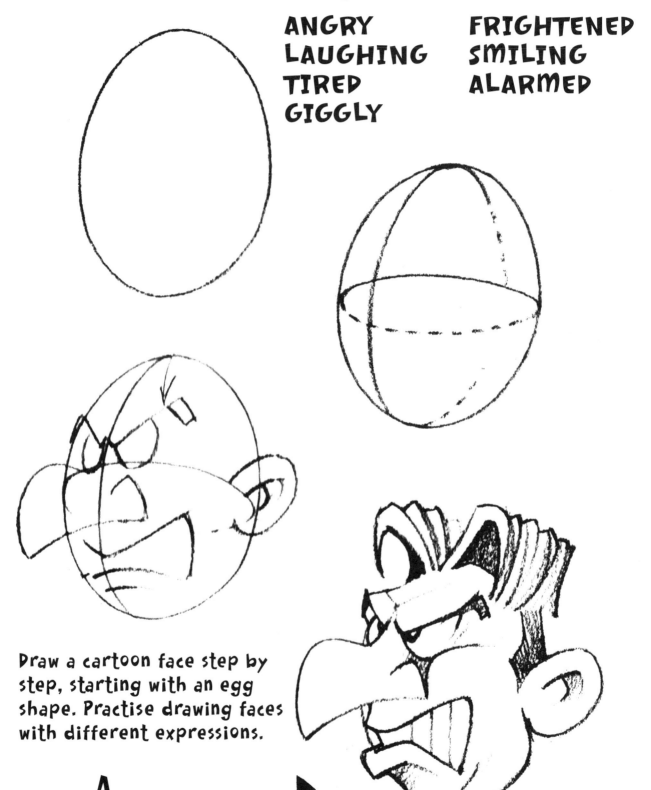

Draw a cartoon face step by step, starting with an egg shape. Practise drawing faces with different expressions.

A ▶

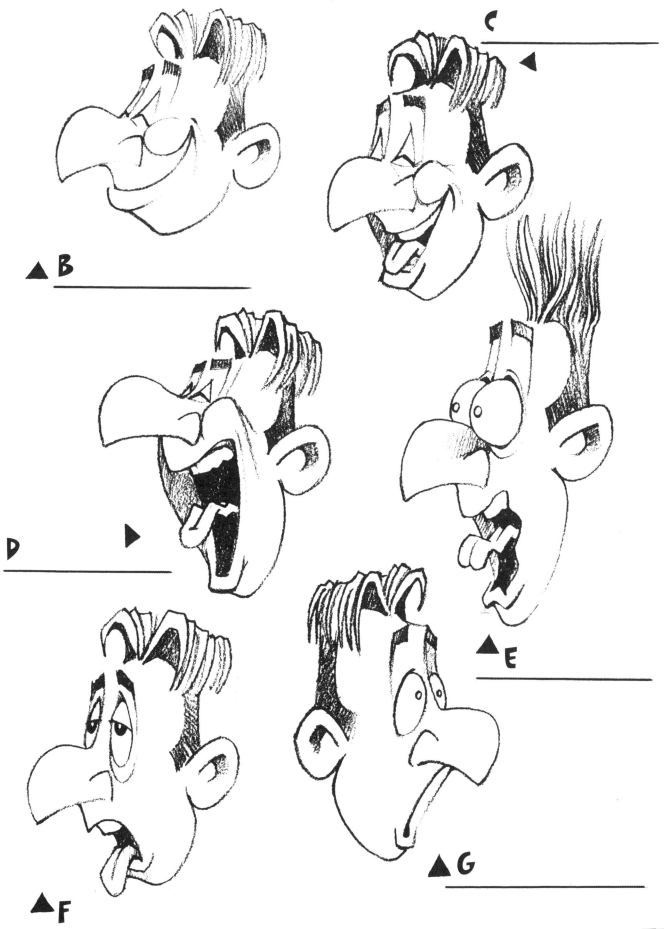

▲ B

C

D ▶

▲ E

▲ F

▲ G

33

Eye, eye!

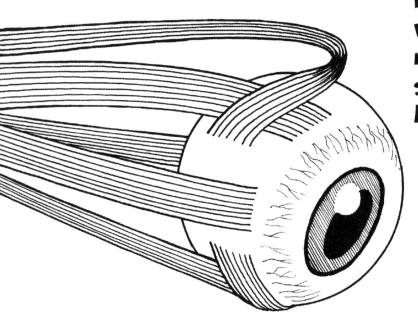

Eyes express your feelings as well as being vital for vision. Eyes may be round or almond-shaped, with long lashes or heavy lids.

Eyes are very distinctive. Can you find the pair that matches mine?

How many pairs of eyes can you find?

Identify organs

Organs are parts of the body with a special job to do.

Write the names of the organs in the correct boxes.

1 HEART
2 SMALL INTESTINE
3 STOMACH
4 BRAIN
5 LARGE INTESTINE
6 OESOPHAGUS (FOODPIPE)
7 KIDNEYS
8 LIVER
9 LUNGS

A

B

C

D

E

F

G

H

I

Colour the picture

Intestine Maze

Find your way through the
maze of the small intestine.

Way in from
the stomach

38

Did you know?
Your small intestine is a thin tube up to 6 metres long. Here much of the goodness in your food passes into your body.

Way out to the large intestine

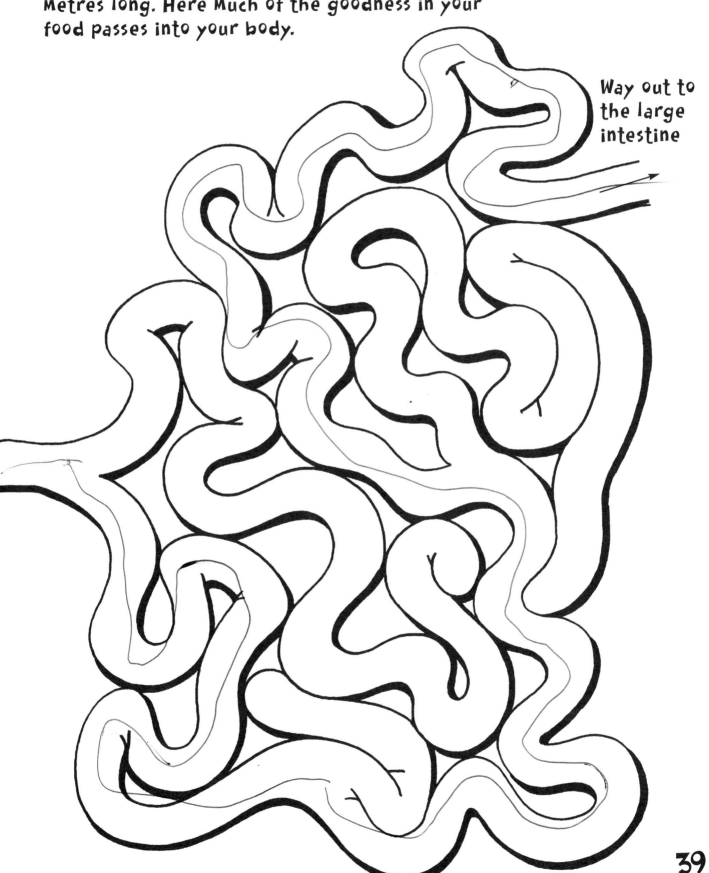

39

Draw the skulls

Copy the skulls onto the opposite page using the grid to help you.

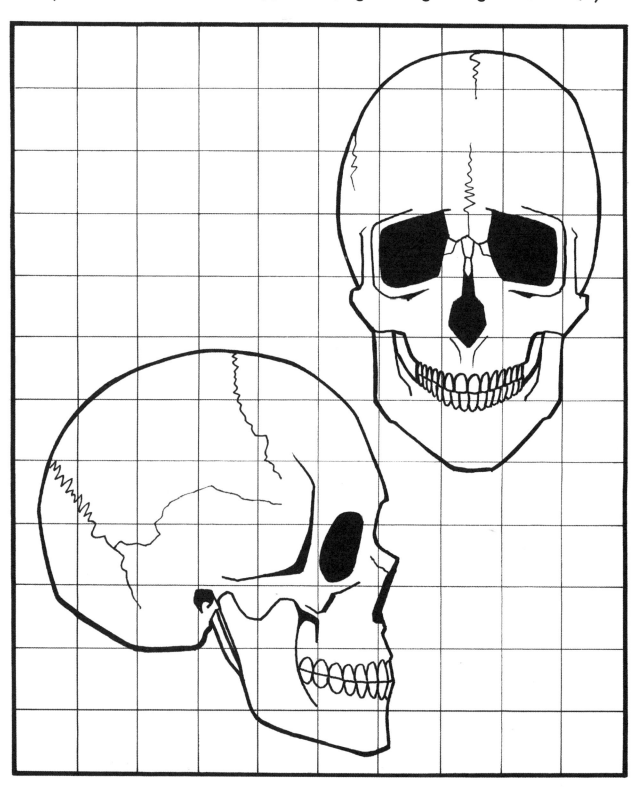

The skull is made up of over 20 bones, joined together at wiggly lines called sutures. The lower jawbone is the only moveable joint.

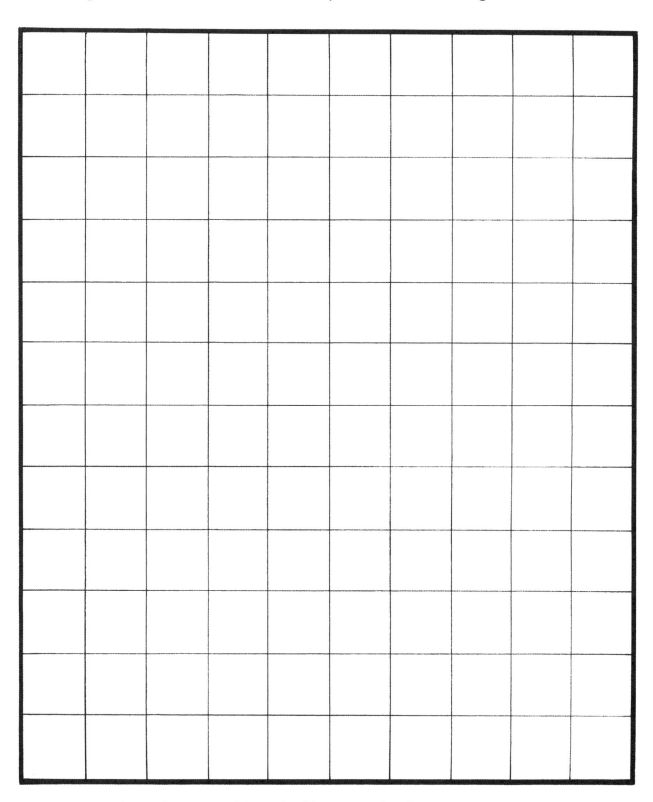

Now try drawing the skull on a blank piece of paper.

Brain centres

Different parts of the brain control your senses and functions such as movement.

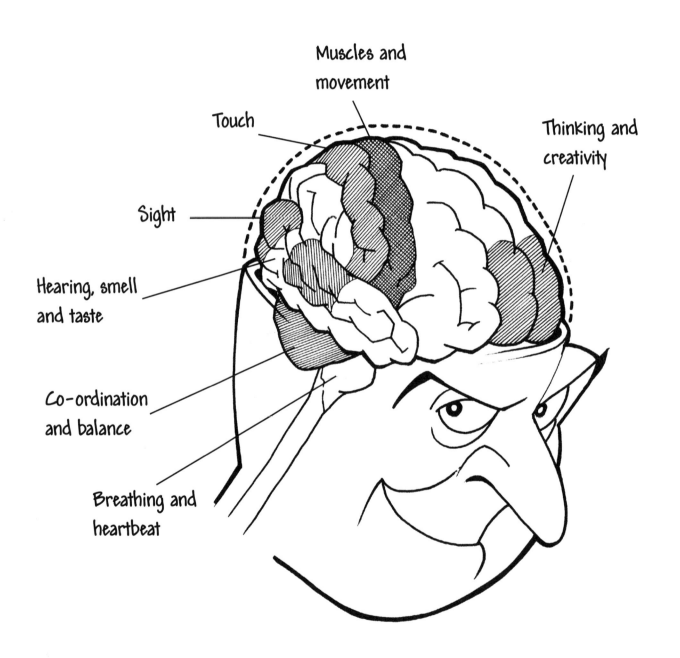

Muscles and movement

Touch

Thinking and creativity

Sight

Hearing, smell and taste

Co-ordination and balance

Breathing and heartbeat

colour the picture

Memory test

Look at these pictures for a minute.
Then turn the page and write down
all the objects you can remember.

43

1

2

3

4

5

6

7

8

9

10

Write down the objects you can remember.

Memory tip:
Making up a story to link all the objects can help you to remember them.

44

Nerve signals

Find the way from your bright idea to the spinal cord.

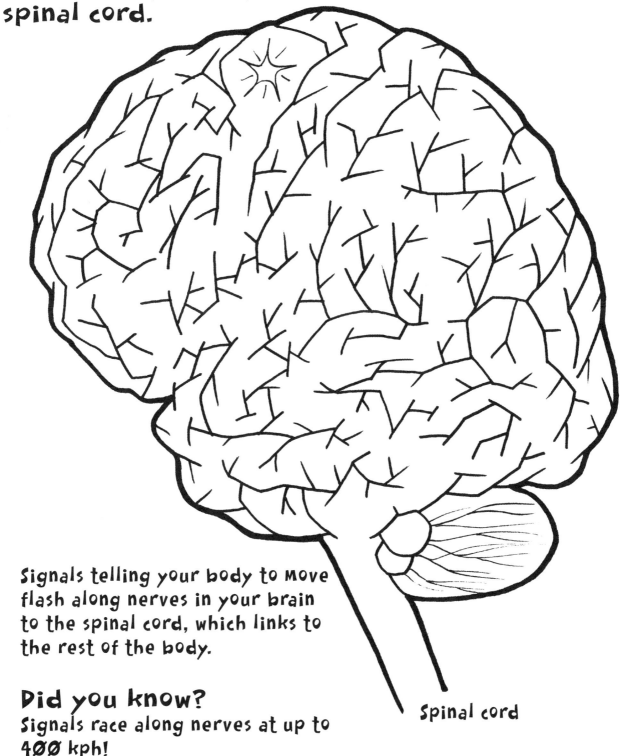

Signals telling your body to move flash along nerves in your brain to the spinal cord, which links to the rest of the body.

Did you know?
Signals race along nerves at up to 400 kph!

Spinal cord

Blood circulation

Colour the blood vessels using the key.

Red = Oxygen-rich blood
Blue = Oxygen-low blood
Yellow = Tissues

Tubes called arteries carry oxygen-rich blood to the body.

Tubes called veins carry blood low in oxygen back to the heart and lungs.

46

Your heart pumps blood
around your body,
delivering oxygen and
nourishment to all parts
that need it, and carrying
away waste.

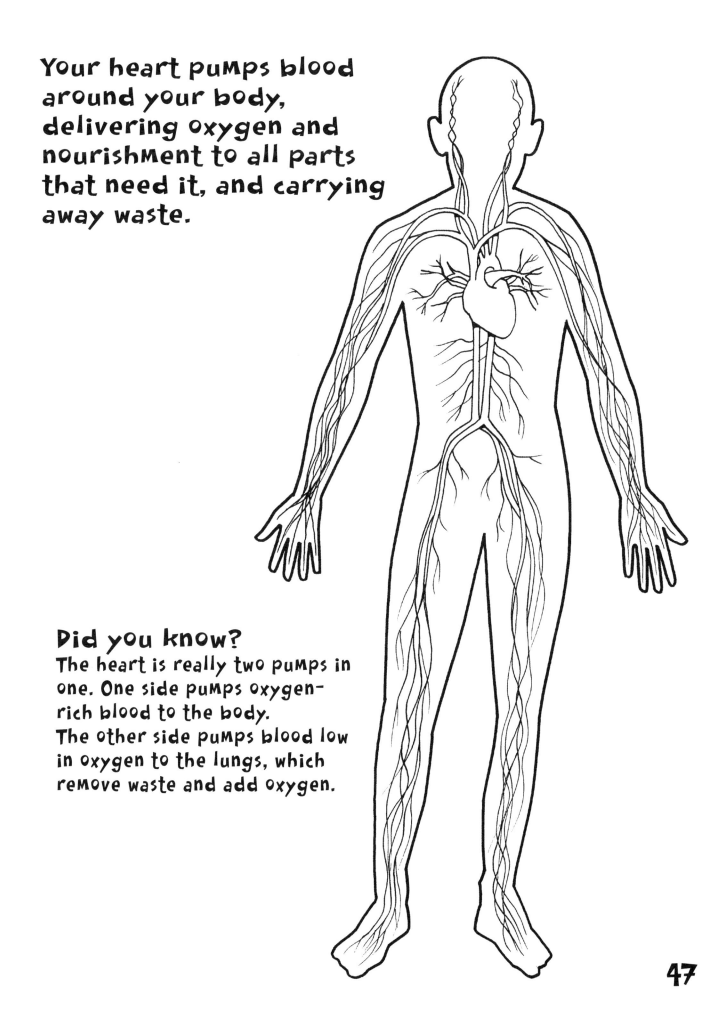

Did you know?
The heart is really two pumps in
one. One side pumps oxygen-
rich blood to the body.
The other side pumps blood low
in oxygen to the lungs, which
remove waste and add oxygen.

Heart

Your heart never stops working night and day, pumping blood around your body.

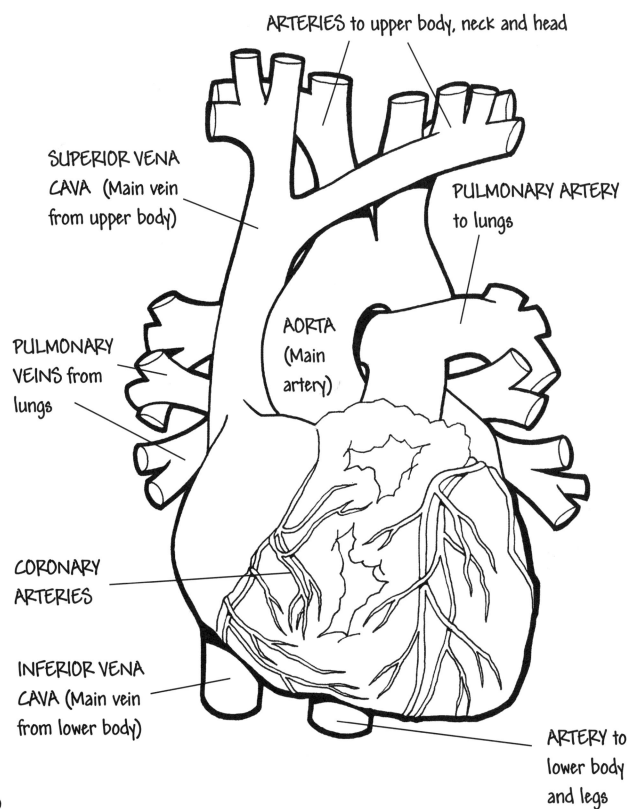

ARTERIES to upper body, neck and head

SUPERIOR VENA CAVA (Main vein from upper body)

PULMONARY ARTERY to lungs

PULMONARY VEINS from lungs

AORTA (Main artery)

CORONARY ARTERIES

INFERIOR VENA CAVA (Main vein from lower body)

ARTERY to lower body and legs

Find the heart words in the wordsearch grid, reading down or across.

ARTERY VENA CORONARY PULMONARY

B	P	U	L	I	V	E	N	A	S
E	U	V	O	A	O	R	T	A	U
Y	L	E	I	R	P	U	J	T	P
J	M	F	N	T	J	N	C	R	E
K	O	I	F	E	L	O	H	V	R
I	N	X	E	R	G	T	W	L	I
L	A	P	R	Y	F	Z	A	H	O
P	R	A	I	J	N	E	O	I	R
Q	Y	C	O	R	O	N	A	R	Y
S	T	V	R	B	B	V	E	I	N

VEIN   AORTA   INFERIOR   SUPERIOR

49

Check your pulse

Every time your heart beats, it sends a surge of blood through your arteries. These little surges are your pulse.

Feel your pulse by pressing two fingers on your wrist below the base of your thumb.

Eating and exercise make your heart beat faster. Time your pulse after doing different activities for two minutes. Record the results below.

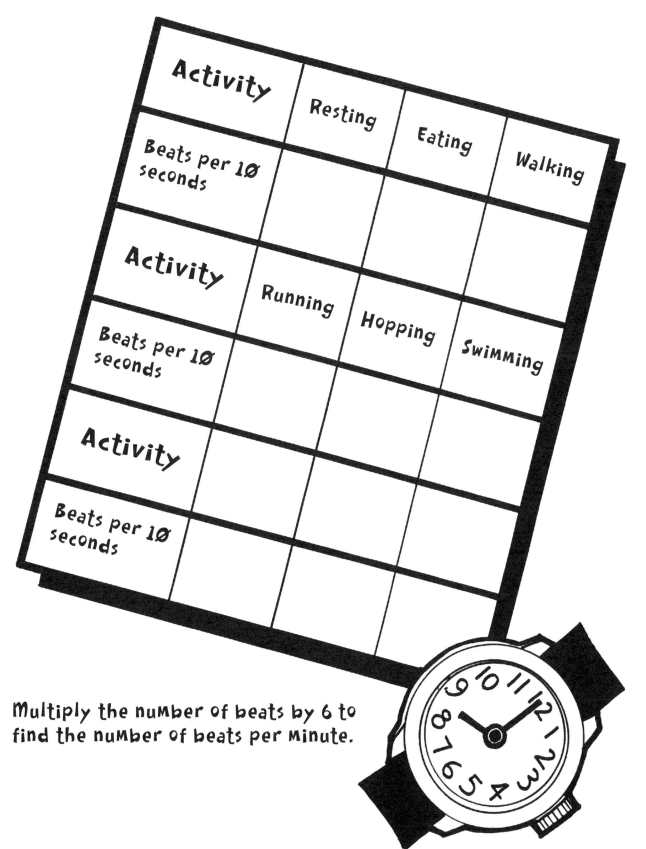

Activity	Resting	Eating	Walking
Beats per 10 seconds			

Activity	Running	Hopping	Swimming
Beats per 10 seconds			

Activity			
Beats per 10 seconds			

Multiply the number of beats by 6 to find the number of beats per minute.

Label the organs

Your body has dozens of organs – not only parts like the heart, lungs and liver, but also your skin and blood.

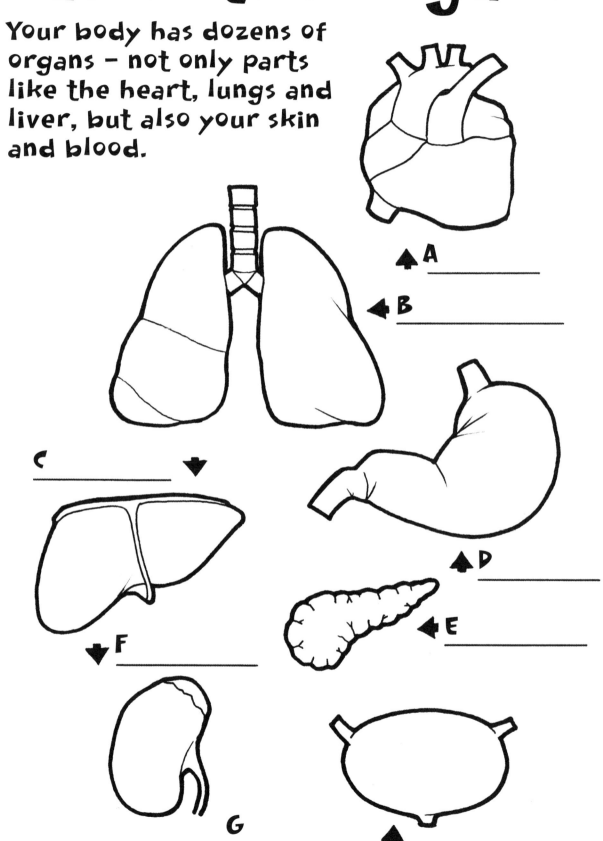

▲A _____

◄B
_____

C _____ ▼

▲D
_____

◄E
_____

▼F _____

G _____ ▲

Write in the names of the organs on the opposite page using the silhouettes below.

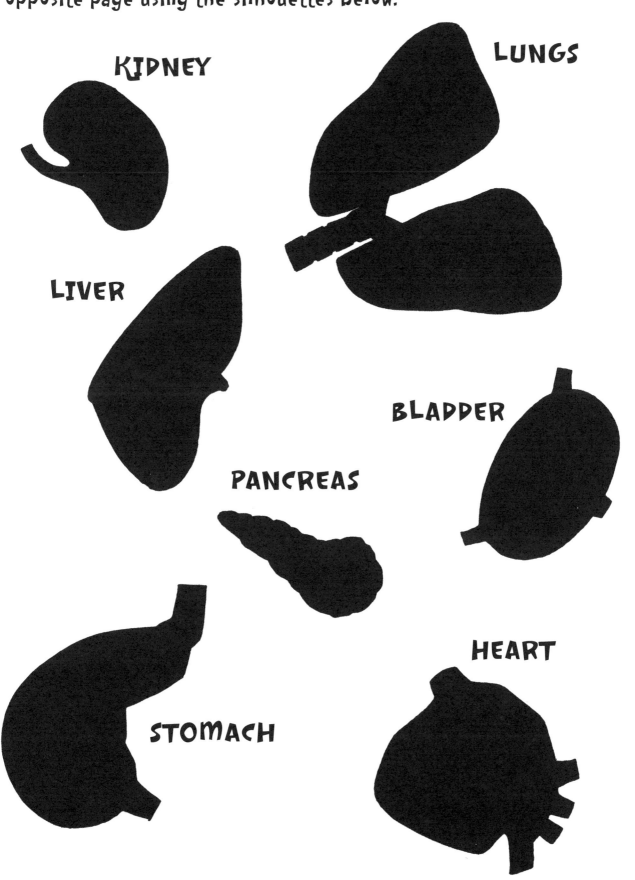

KIDNEY

LUNGS

LIVER

BLADDER

PANCREAS

STOMACH

HEART

Spot the twin

Can you find my identical twin? Clue – check the freckles!

Identical twins look almost the same – but look very closely and you May spot the difference!

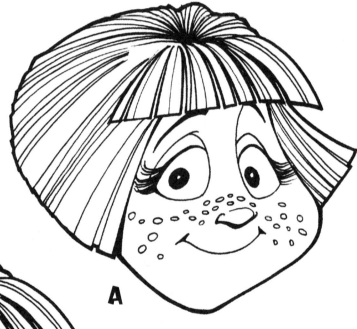

A

B

C

D

E

Did you know?
Non-identical twins
are twice as common
as identical twins.

F

Vein Maze

A network of tubes called veins returns blood to the heart from the body.

Which of these veins leads to the heart?

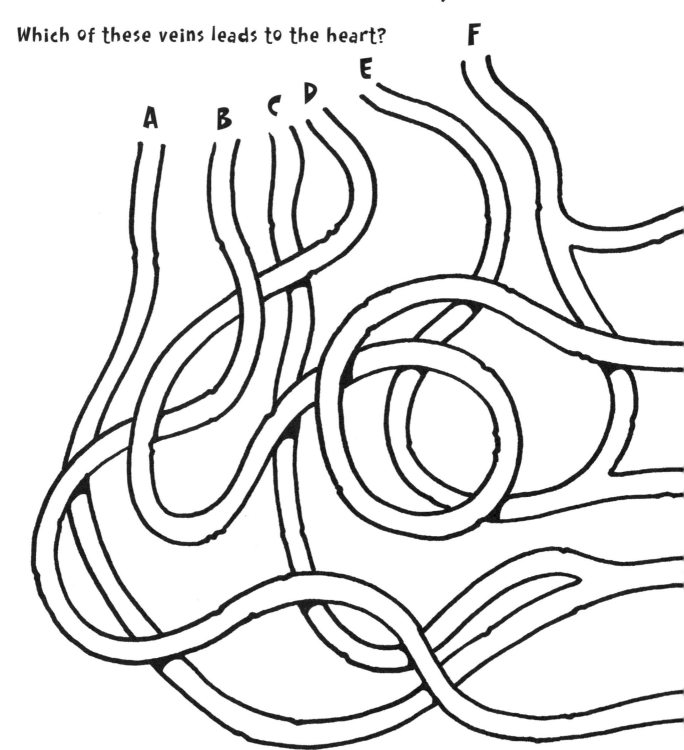

Your heart is about the size of your fist.

Did you know?
The blood in your veins looks reddish-purple, because it is low in oxygen.

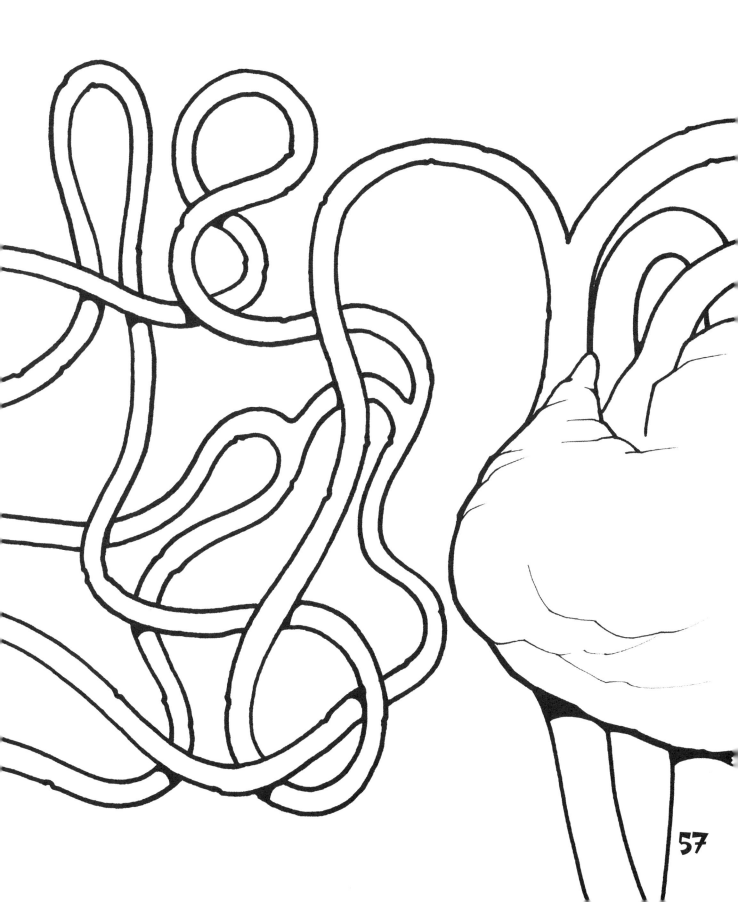

Growing up

Your body has changed a lot since you were little.

Photocopy photos of yourself as a baby, as a toddler and at different ages, and stick them in the frames.

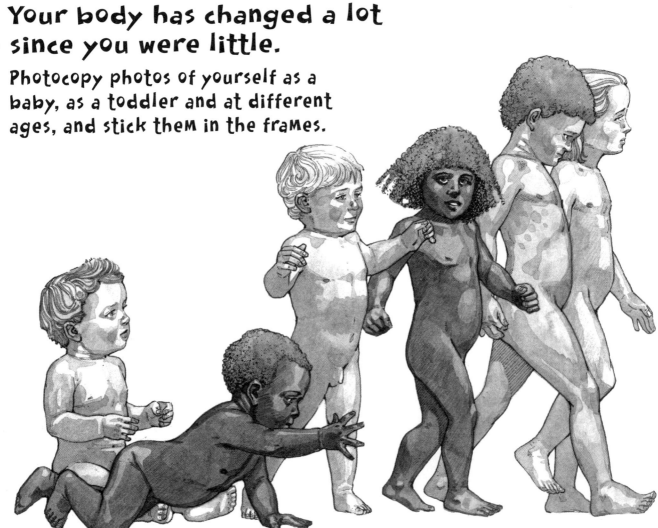

How much do you grow each year? Ask an
adult to measure you on your birthday
each year. Mark your height on a wall or
on a large piece of paper.

59

Find the teeth

The top or crown of your teeth is covered with super-hard enamel. The soft pulp inside is supplied with blood. The root anchors the tooth in your jaw.

Colour the tooth using the key:

Y: Yellow
P: Pink
O: Orange
R: Red

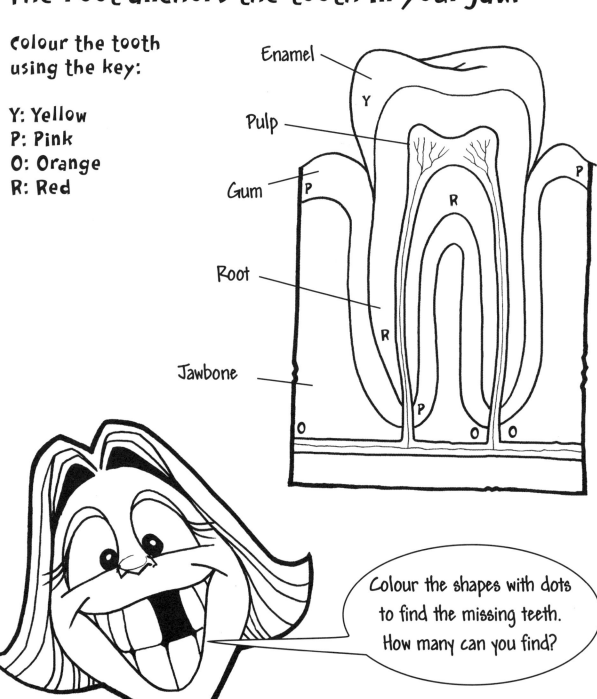

Colour the shapes with dots to find the missing teeth. How many can you find?

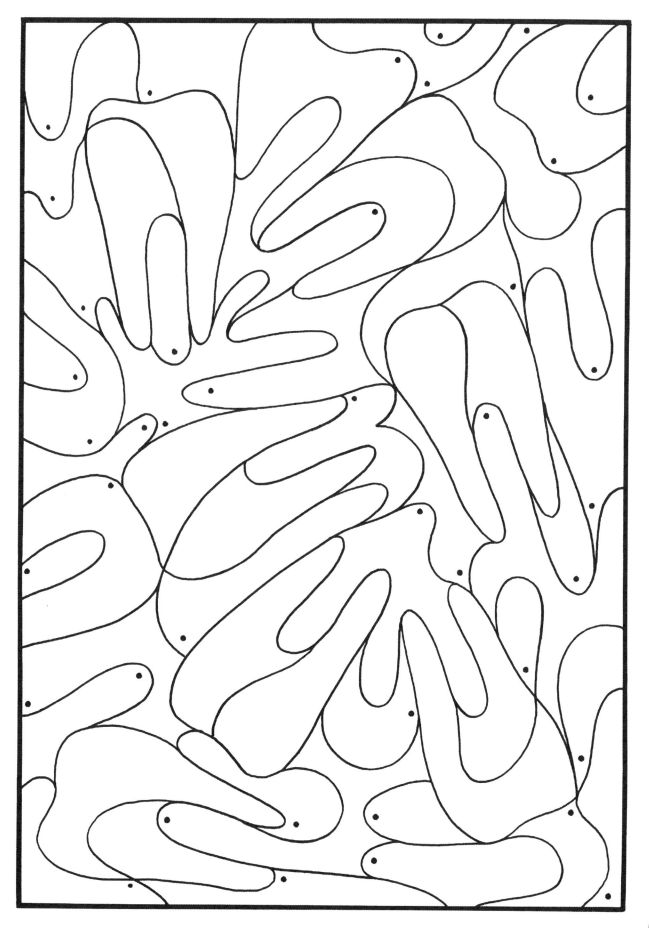

61

Gappy grins

A B

C D

E F

Which of the lost teeth fits where?
Match the letters on the teeth to the numbers on the gaps.

Did you know?
You have two sets of teeth in your lifetime. The first set or 'milk teeth' fall out and are replaced by your adult set.

complete the faces

**The two sides of a face
never match exactly.**
Draw in the other sides of these faces.

Did you know?
When you look in a
mirror the image is
reversed. So you never
see yourself exactly as
others see you!

Body crossword

Your body contains literally hundreds of body parts. Parts such as the head contain many smaller parts, such as eyes, ears and nose.

Put the body words in the grid.

Hint: Count the letters. Start with the longest words.

MUSCLE, HEAD, SHOULDER, CHEST, ELBOW, EAR, WRIST, FINGER, HAIR, ARM, HAND, SHIN, NECK, NOSE, ANKLE, KNEE

f i n

How many body parts can you name on your head?

g e r

How many body parts can you name beginning with S?

67

Body framework

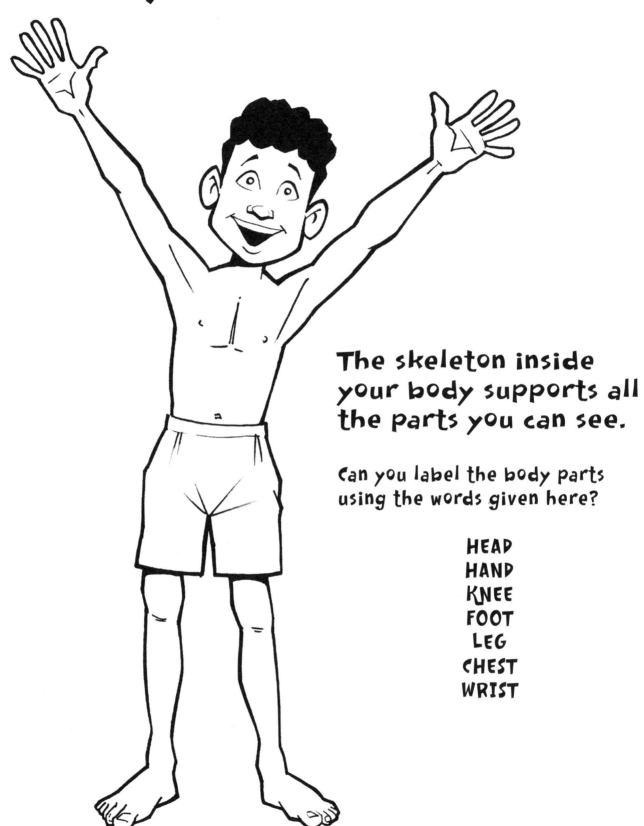

The skeleton inside your body supports all the parts you can see.

Can you label the body parts using the words given here?

HEAD
HAND
KNEE
FOOT
LEG
CHEST
WRIST

Your skeleton contains bones of
different shapes and sizes. Some
are large, others are tiny.

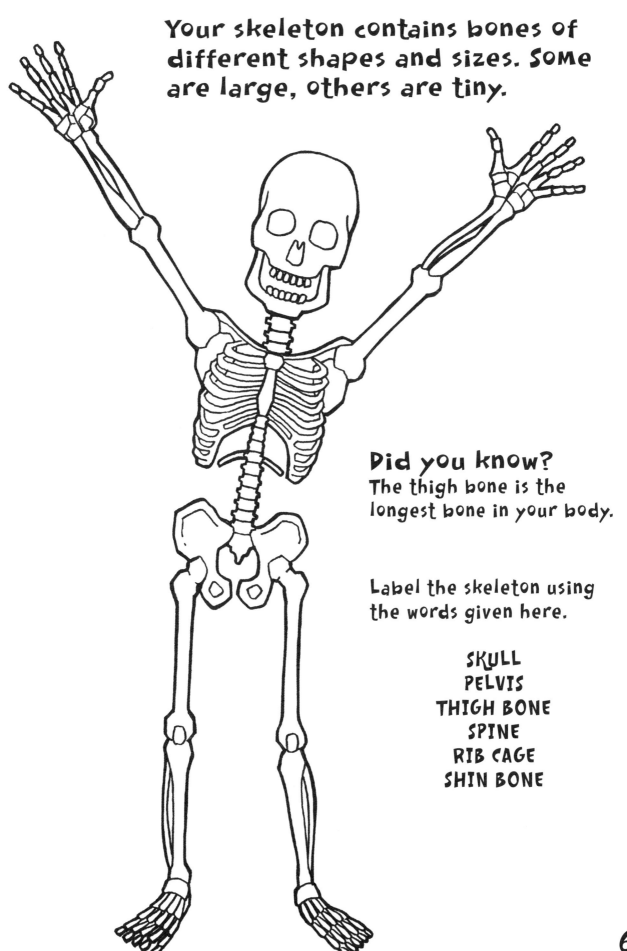

Did you know?
The thigh bone is the
longest bone in your body.

Label the skeleton using
the words given here.

SKULL
PELVIS
THIGH BONE
SPINE
RIB CAGE
SHIN BONE

Match the skeletons

The adult skeleton contains about 206 bones. The smallest bones are in your ears!

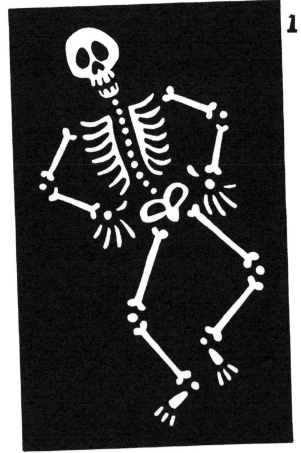

Find two skeletons that match exactly.

3

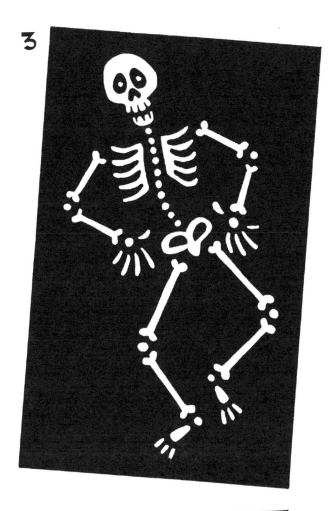

4

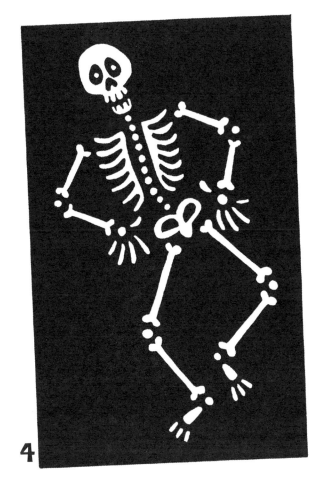

5

6

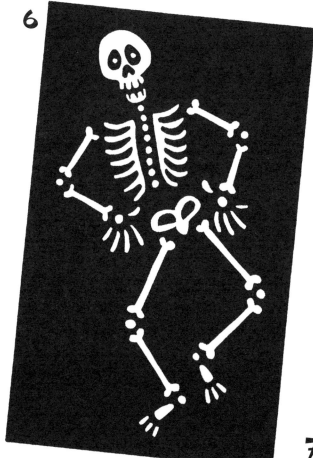

Draw your own hand

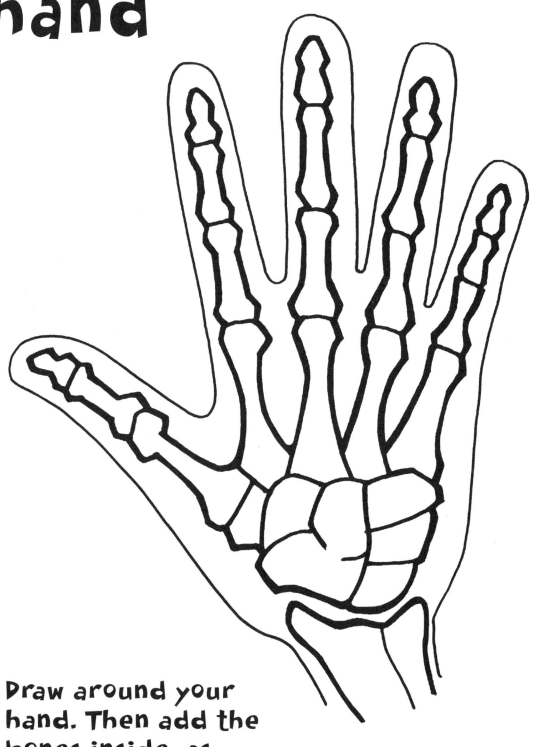

Draw around your hand. Then add the bones inside, as shown on this page.

Did you know?

Each of your hands has 27 bones. These small bones allow you to carry out all sorts of actions, such as gripping, stroking and threading a needle.

Funny faces

Your face has many muscles, which allows you to pull all sorts of funny faces. How many faces can you pull?

Colour in the faces on the next six pages. Cut along the lines to separate the top, middle and bottom parts of the faces. Swap the strips to make weird and wacky faces that have never been seen before!

(If you don't want to cut the book, trace the pictures instead.)

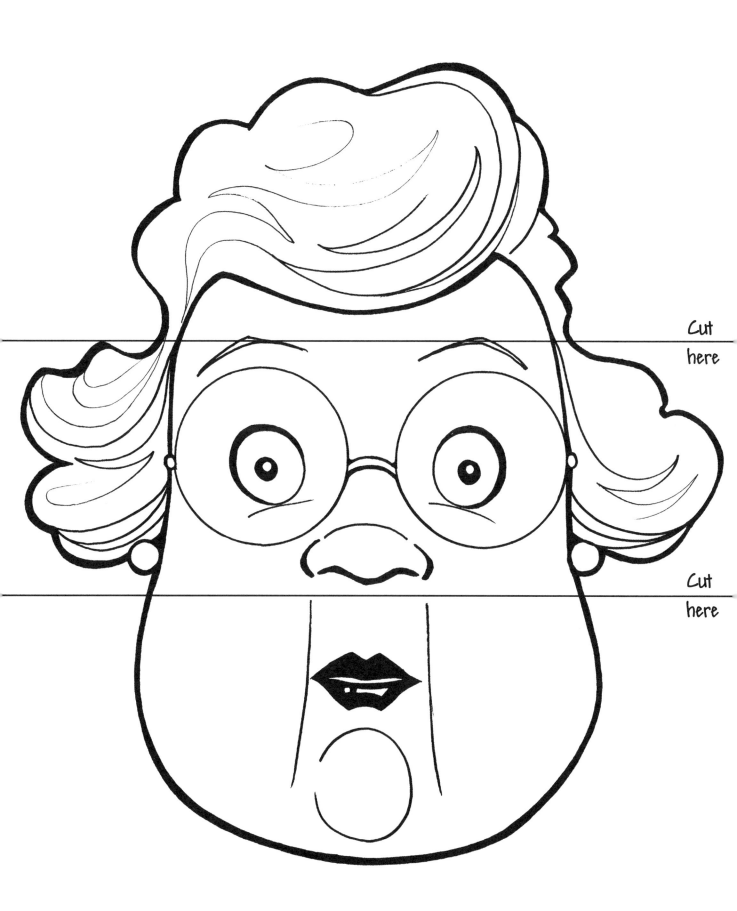

Cut here

Cut here

77

78

80

Parts of the face

Find the words for parts of the face hidden in the wordsearch grid.

HAIR LIPS NOSE EYELASHES EYEBROWS

CHIN MOUTH EARS NOSTRILS

G	Y	B	L	V	N	O	S	E	H
L	H	A	I	R	L	J	T	Y	T
J	T	C	P	R	N	Y	S	E	N
P	I	R	S	J	C	B	L	L	m
W	Q	E	F	T	X	P	I	A	O
N	E	Y	E	B	R	O	W	S	U
A	W	U	A	N	W	C	E	H	T
L	P	H	R	I	E	H	O	E	H
D	N	O	S	T	R	I	L	S	E
C	Z	B	P	A	O	N	U	A	O

spot the difference

Spot seven differences between these two drawings.

Did you know?
Your rib cage protects your digestive system, as well as delicate parts such as your heart and lungs.

The five senses

Your five senses are sight, smell, hearing, taste and touch. Sight is the most important sense.

This is what you would look like if your body parts were in proportion to the space in your brain that receives sense information from each part.

colour the picture.

Draw your version

Did you know?
The most touch-sensitive areas are your lips, your tongue, the palms of your hands and the soles of your feet.

Dotty hands

Having a thumb allows you to grip all sorts of objects, from a pea to a pencil. Monkeys and apes also have thumbs, which helps them to climb trees.

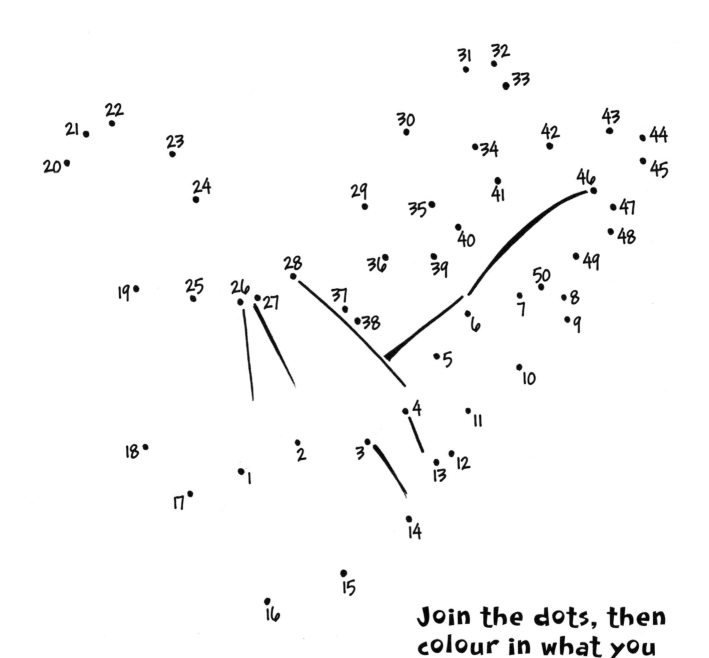

Join the dots, then colour in what you have drawn.

How many left hands and how many right hands can you find on this page?

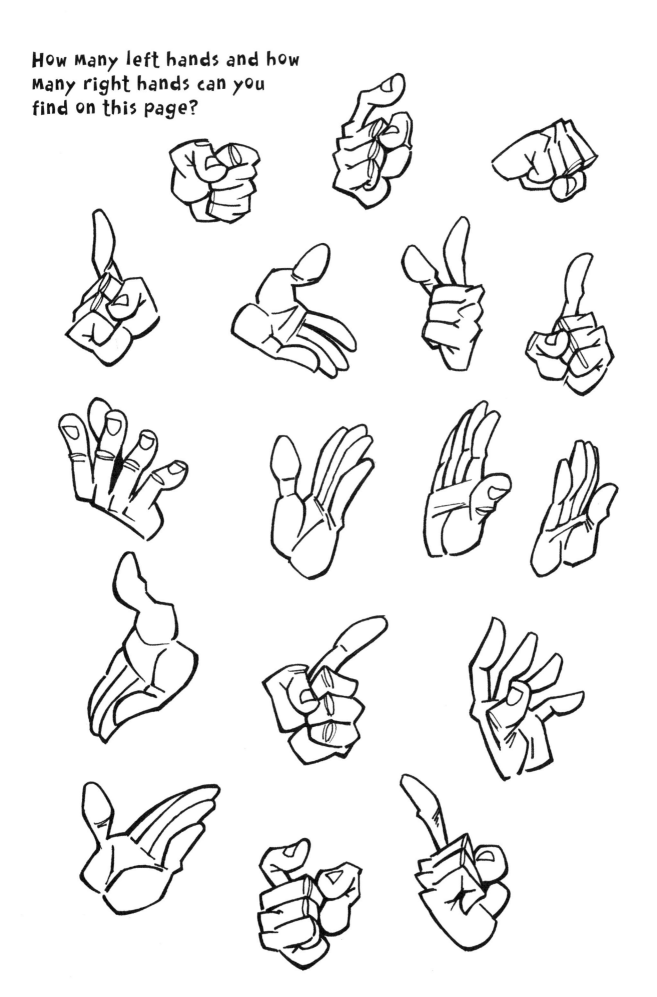

Bone crossword

Fit the bone names in the grid.
Hint: count the letters. Fill in the shortest and the longest words.

TIBIA RADIUS SKULL CLAVICLE
~~HUMERUS~~ FEMUR PELVIS FIBULA
SCAPULA PATELLA RIBS TARSALS
STERNUM PHALANGES

Did you know?

The humerus and radius are arm bones. The femur, patella, tibia and tarsals are in your legs and feet. The phalanges are your toe and finger bones.

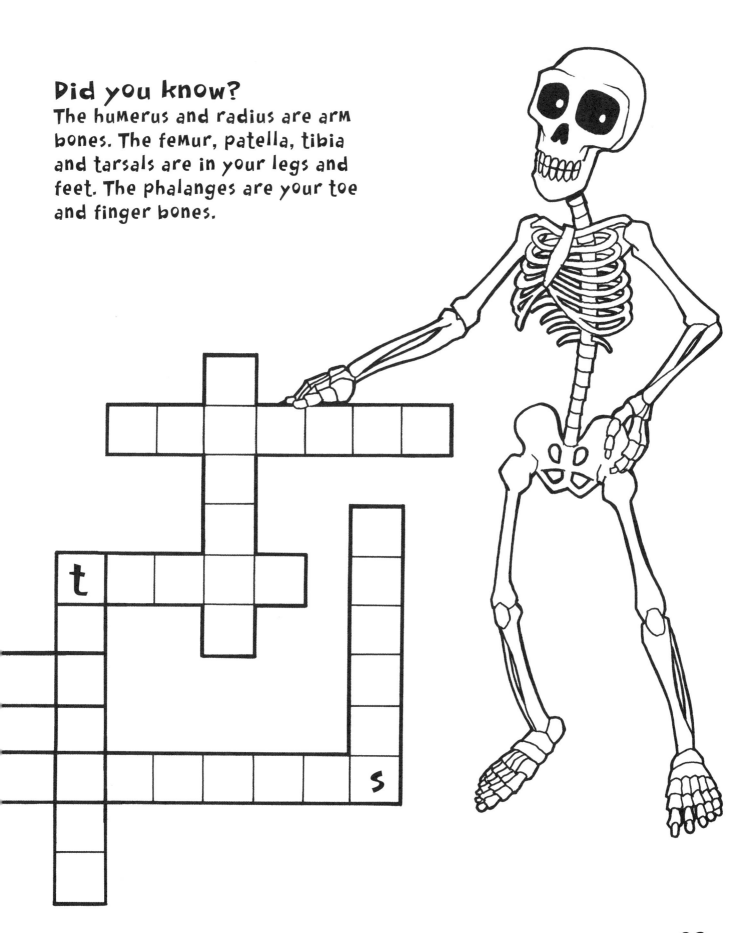

Draw the skeletons

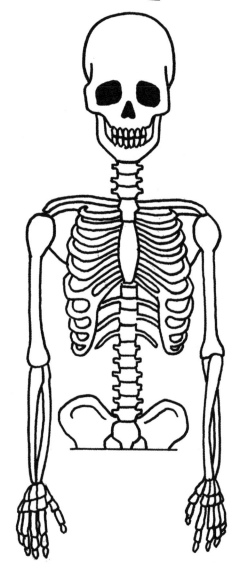

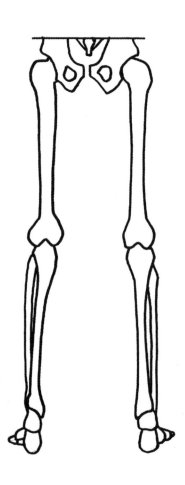

90

Did you know?
Some of your bones are long and thin, others are flat or rounded. All are tough and strong!

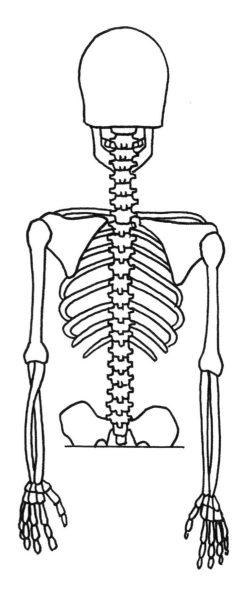

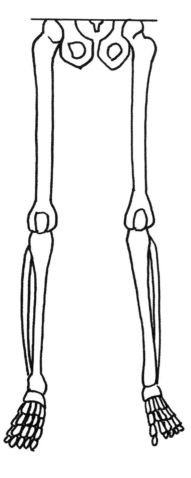

Your neck and spine are made up of 26 small, knobby bones called vertebrae.

Answers

Pages 10-11: Match the organs

1 Kidney, 2 Brain, 3 Intestines, 4 Lungs, 5 Heart, 6 Stomach,
7 Spleen, 8 Pancreas

Page 17: Match the food type

Bread = Carbohydrates, Milk = Calcium, Meat = Protein,
Fruit = Vitamins and minerals, Chips = Fat and sugar

Page 22: Windpipe maze

Page 24-25: Digestive puzzle

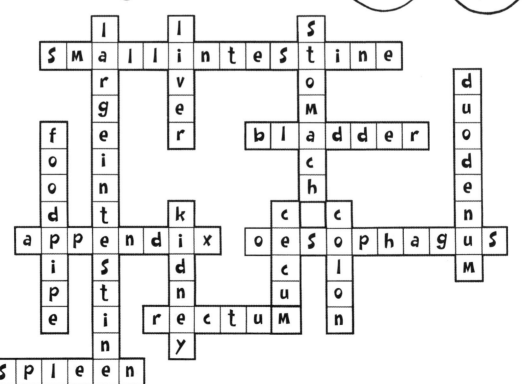

Page 26: Sudoku

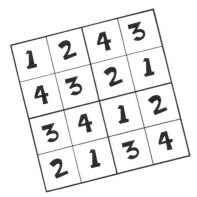

Page 27: Digestive Maze

Page 38-29: Digestive system

There are at least 40 words of three letters or more that can be made. Here are some of the more interesting ones:

3 letters: dig, tie, sit, get, set, vet, dim, sty, met, tee, yes

4 letters: vest, ties, tide, side, seed, meet, digs, time, diet, miss

5 letters: sieve, stems, styes, misty, times, visit, sissy, midge, messy

6 letters: devise, desist, detest, smites, tester, midget, digits

8 letters: vegetist, misgives, vestiges, mistiest

You may have to look some of these up in the dictionary.

Pages 32-33: Facial expressions

A Angry, B Smiling, C Giggly, D Laughing, E Frightened, F Tired, G Alarmed

Pages 34-35: Eye, eye!   11 pairs.

Pages 36-37: Identify organs

A4, B6, C9, D1, E8, F3, G7, H2, I5

Pages 38-39: Intestine Maze

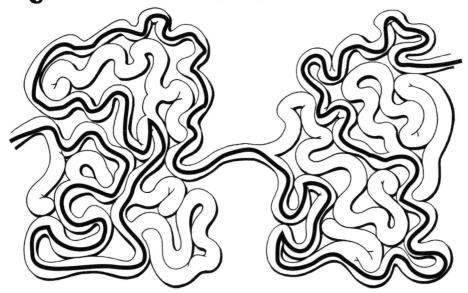

Page 45: Nerve signals

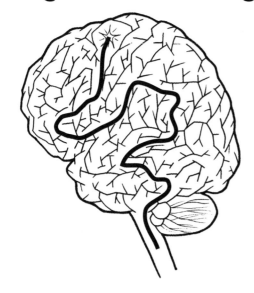

Page 49: Heart wordsearch

B	P	U	L	I	V	E	N	A	S
E	U	V	O	A	O	R	T	A	U
Y	L	E	I	R	P	U	J	T	P
J	M	F	N	T	J	N	C	R	E
K	O	I	F	E	L	O	H	V	R
I	N	X	E	R	G	T	W	L	I
L	A	D	R	Y	F	Z	A	H	O
D	R	A	I	J	N	E	O	I	R
Q	Y	C	O	R	O	N	A	R	Y
S	T	V	R	B	B	V	E	I	N

Pages 52-53: Label the organs

A Heart, B Lungs, C Liver, D Stomach, E Pancreas, F Kidney, G Bladder

Pages 54-55: Spot the twin E.

Pages 56–57: Vein Maze D.

Page 61: How many teeth? 7.

Pages 62–63: Gappy grins

A1, B6, C5, D2. E3, F4

Pages 66–67: Body crossword

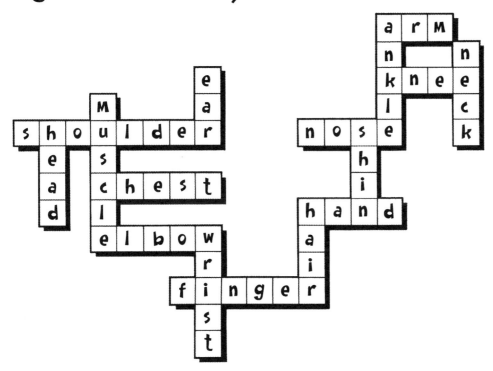

Pages 68–69: Body framework

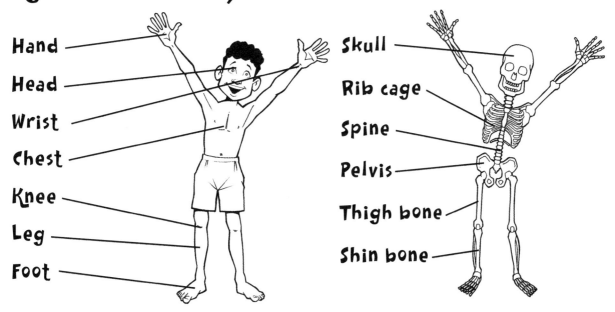

Hand
Head
Wrist
Chest
Knee
Leg
Foot

Skull
Rib cage
Spine
Pelvis
Thigh bone
Shin bone

Pages 70-71: Match the skeletons 2 and 4.

Page 81: Parts of the face wordsearch

G	Y	B	L	V	N	O	S	E	H
L	H	A	I	R	L	J	T	Y	T
J	T	C	P	R	N	Y	S	E	N
E	I	R	S	J	C	B	L	L	M
W	Q	E	F	T	X	P	I	A	O
N	E	Y	E	B	R	O	W	S	U
A	W	U	A	N	W	C	E	H	T
L	P	H	R	I	E	H	O	E	H
D	N	O	S	T	R	I	L	S	E
C	Z	B	P	A	O	N	U	A	O

Pages 82-83: Spot the difference

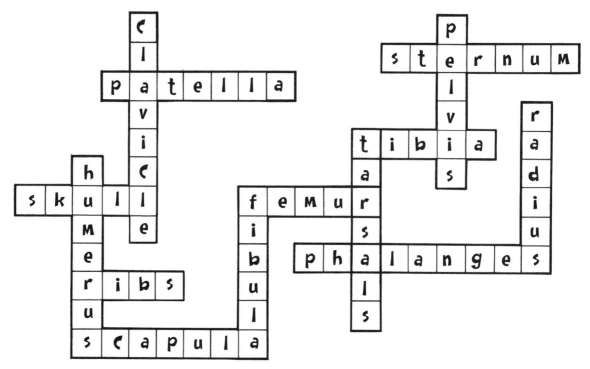

Page 87: How many hands? 9 right and 8 left.

Pages 88-89: Bone crossword